Piano Recital Showcase

12 FAVORITE PIECES CAREFULLY SELECTED FOR ELEMENTARY LEVEL

CONTENTS

ISBN 978-1-4234-5661-2

HAL•LEONARD®
CORPORATION

7777 W. BLUEMOUND RD. P.O. BOX 13819 MILWAUKEE, WI 53213

In Australia Contact:
Hal Leonard Australia Pty. Ltd.
4 Lentara Court
Cheltenham, Victoria, 3192 Australia
Email: ausadmin@halleonard.com.au

Visit Hal Leonard Online at
www.halleonard.com

In My Dreams

Words and Music by
Jennifer Linn

Peacefully (♩ = 116)

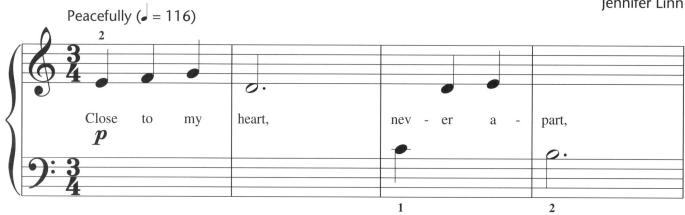

Close to my heart, nev - er a - part,

p

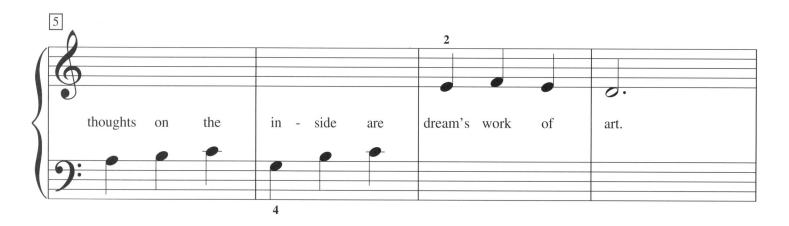

thoughts on the in - side are dream's work of art.

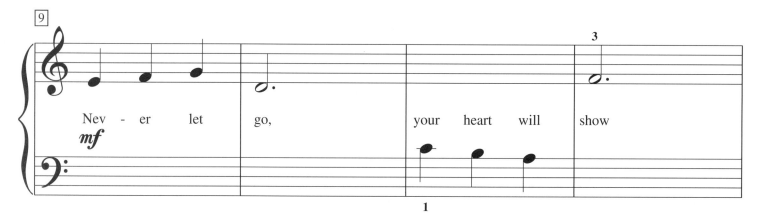

Nev - er let go, your heart will show

mf

Accompaniment (Student plays one octave higher than written.)

Peacefully (♩ = 116)

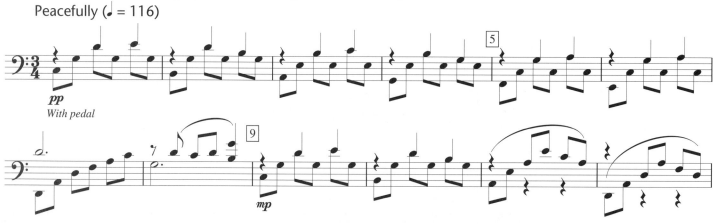

pp

With pedal

mp

noth - ing's im - pos - si - ble where dreams can grow.

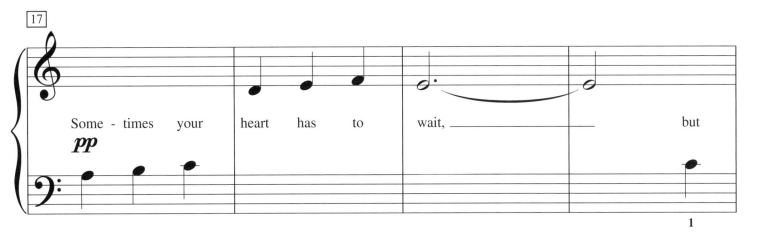

Some - times your heart has to wait, _____ but

pp

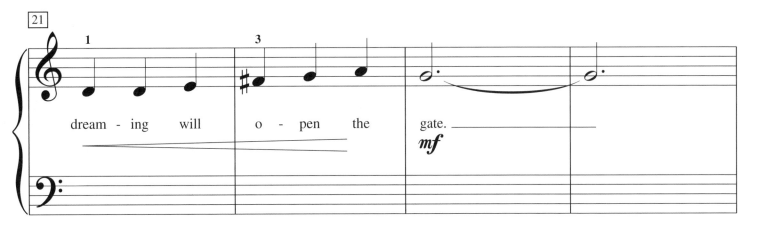

dream - ing will o - pen the gate. _____

mf

3

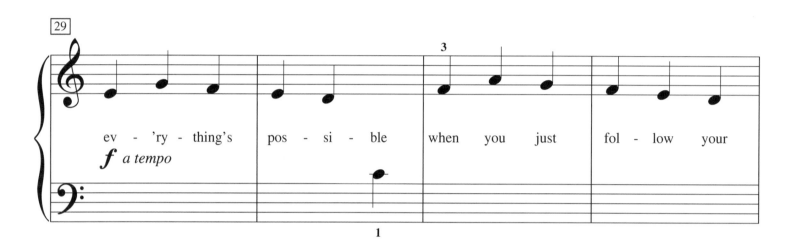

4

Ocean Breezes

By Mona Rejino

Gently flowing (♩ = 126-138)

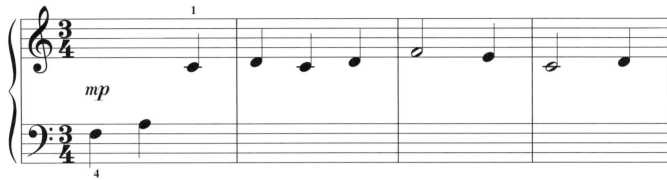

As Solo, hold down the damper pedal throughout.

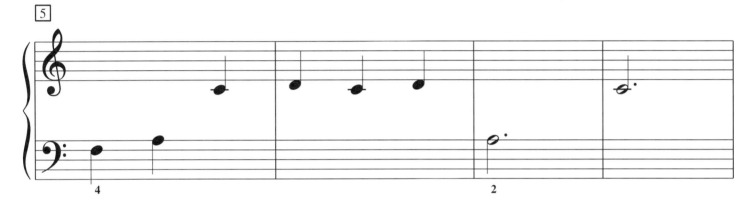

Accompaniment (Student plays one octave higher than written.)

Gently flowing (♩ = 126-138)

p

With pedal

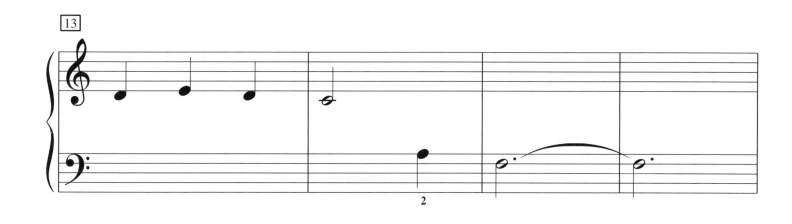

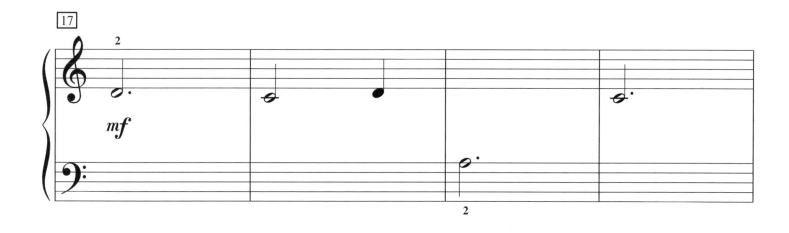

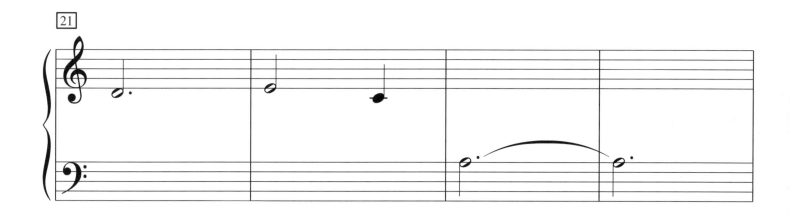

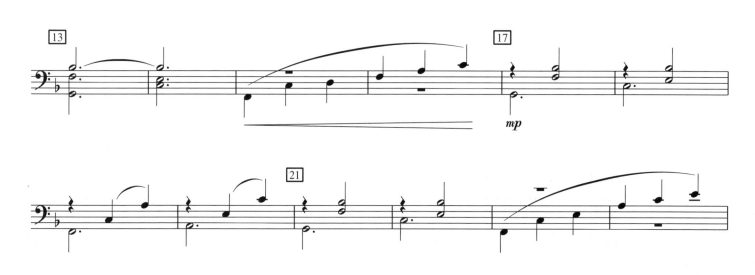

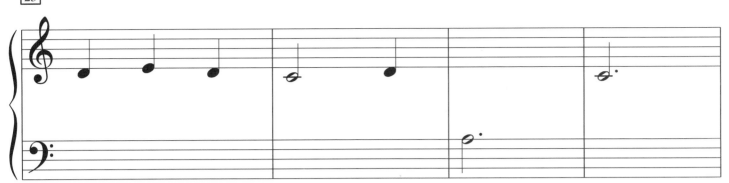

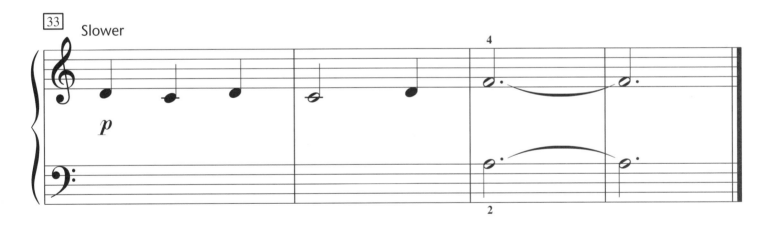

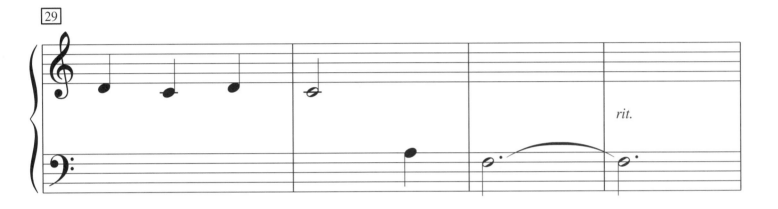

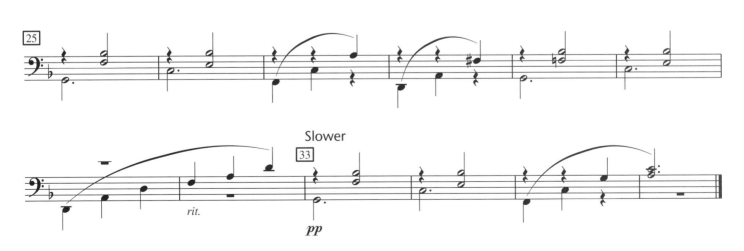

Japanese Garden

By Jennifer Linn

Peacefully (♩ = 88)

As Solo, play one octave higher and hold down damper pedal throughout.

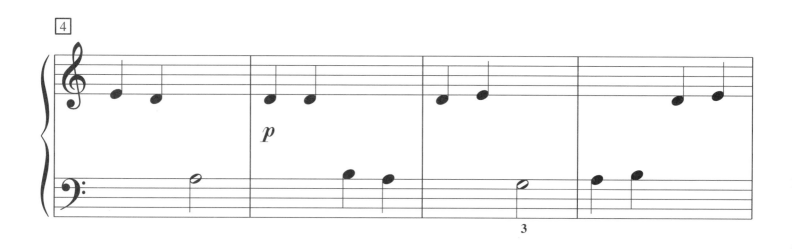

Accompaniment (Student plays as written.)

Peacefully (♩ = 88)

pp throughout

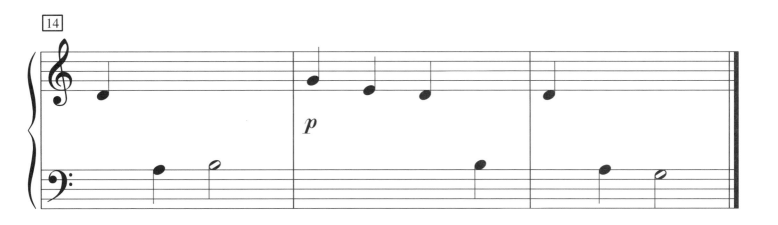

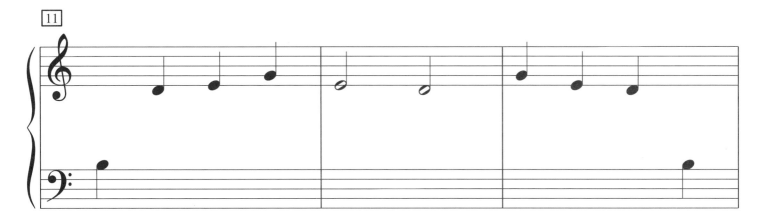

9

Jazz Jig

By Phillip Keveren

With driving energy ($\quarternote$ = 184)

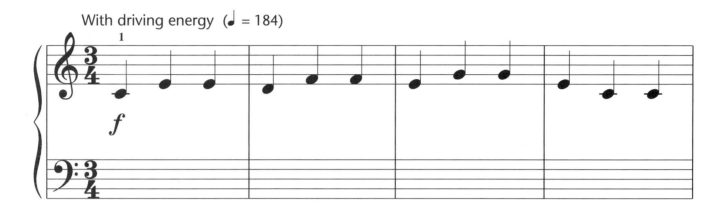

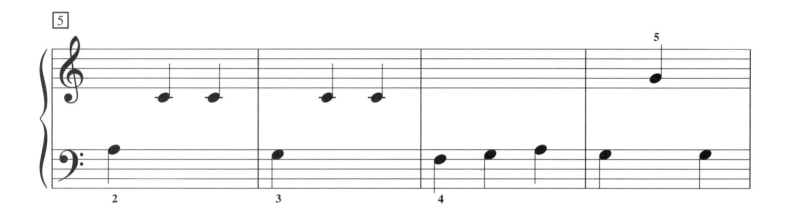

Accompaniment (Student plays one octave higher than written.)

With driving energy ($\quarternote$ = 184)

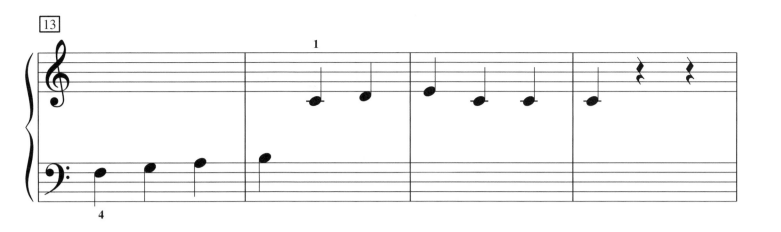

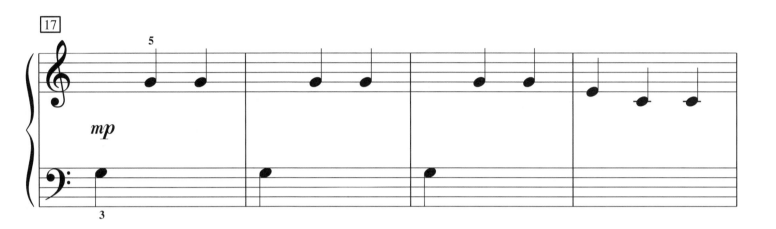

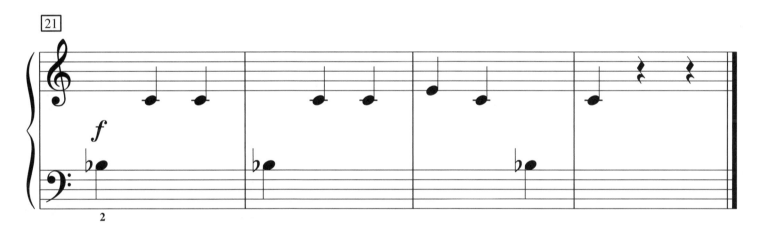

Sledding Fun

Words and Music by
Peggy Otwell

Smoothly (♩ = 184-200)

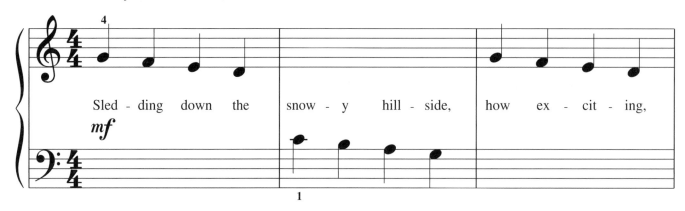

Sled - ding down the snow - y hill - side, how ex - cit - ing,

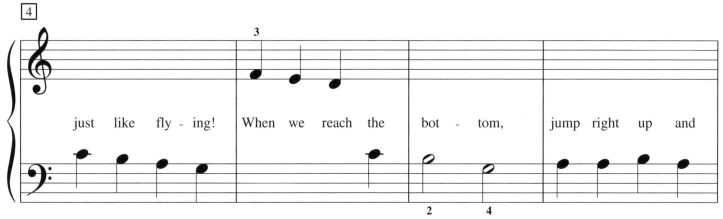

just like fly - ing! When we reach the bot - tom, jump right up and

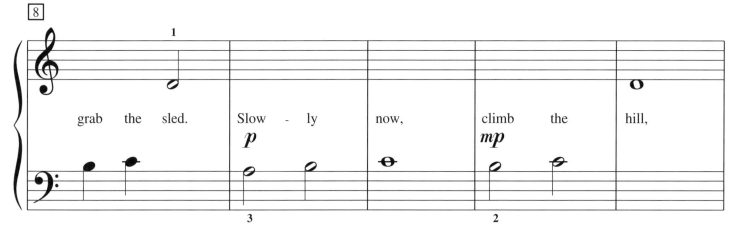

grab the sled. Slow - ly now, climb the hill,

Accompaniment (Student plays one octave higher than written.)

Smoothly (♩ = 184-200)

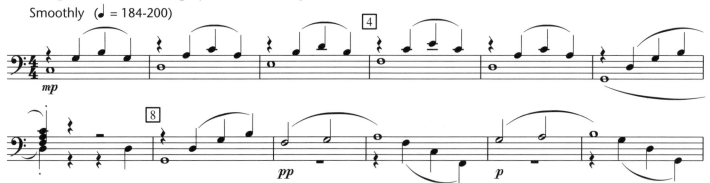

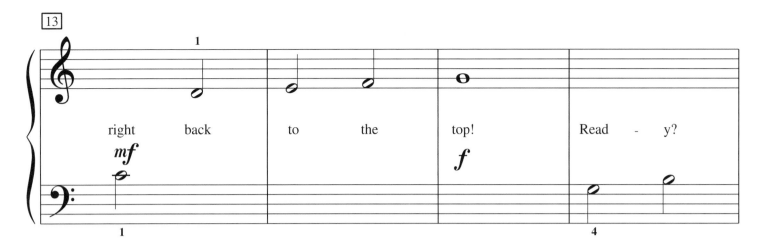

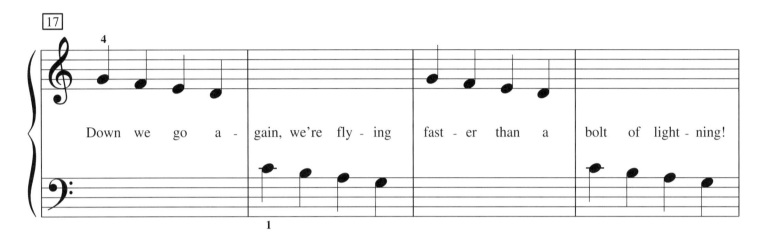

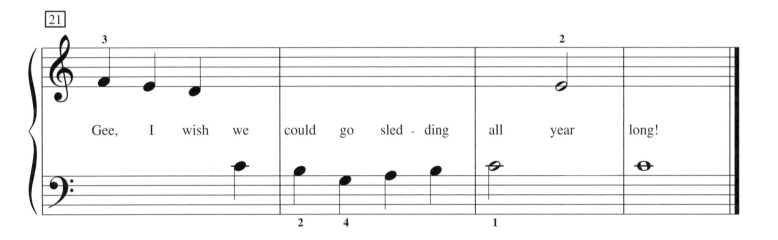

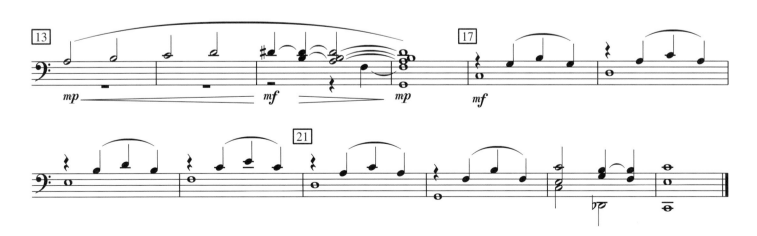

B.B.'s Boogie

By Bill Boyd

With spirit (♩ = 160-168)

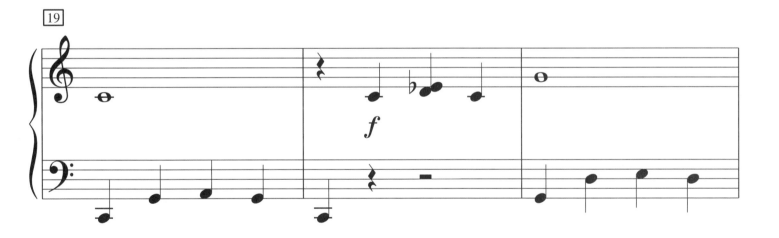

15

Joyful Bells

By Jennifer Linn

Majestic (♩ = 126)

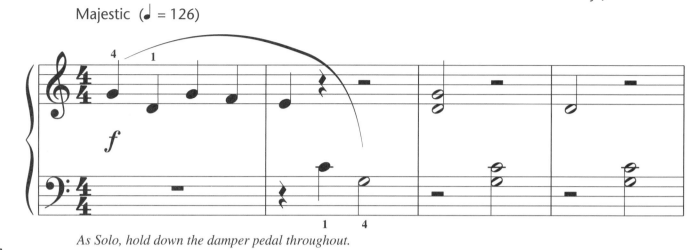

As Solo, hold down the damper pedal throughout.

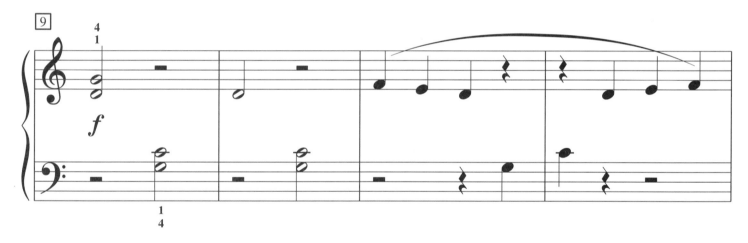

Accompaniment (Student plays one octave higher than written.)

Majestic (♩ = 126)

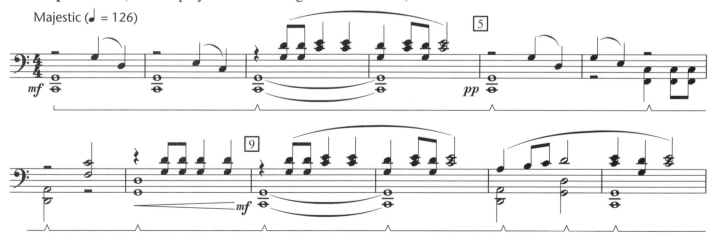

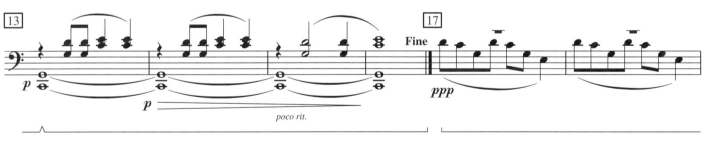

Lost Treasure

By Mona Rejino

Smoothly flowing ($\quarternote$ = 116-120)

Accompaniment (Student plays one octave higher than written.)

Smoothly flowing ($\quarternote$ = 116-120)

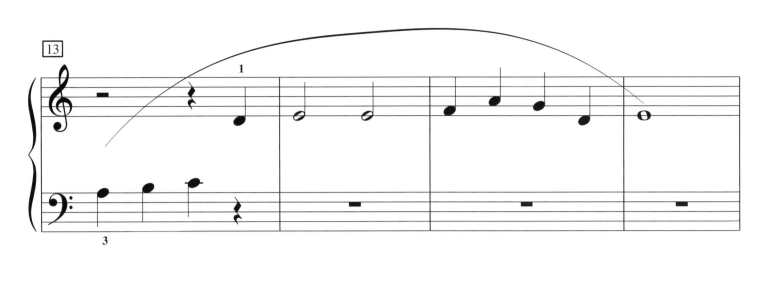

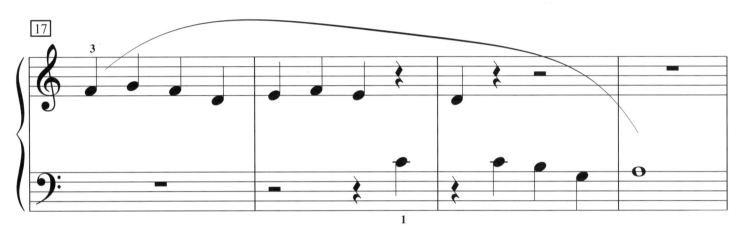

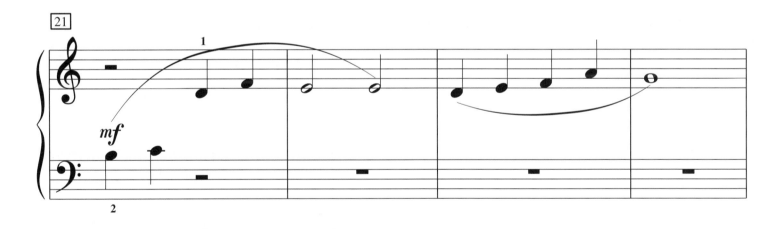

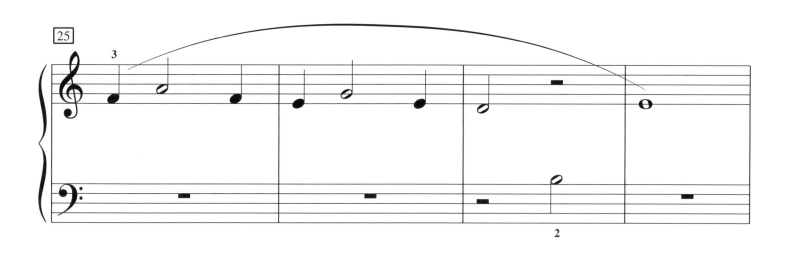

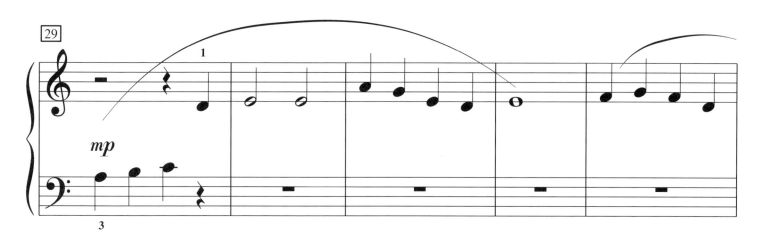

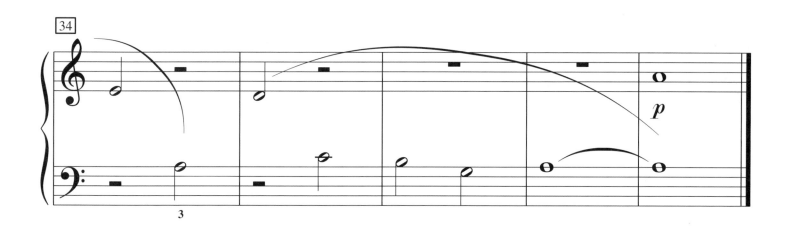

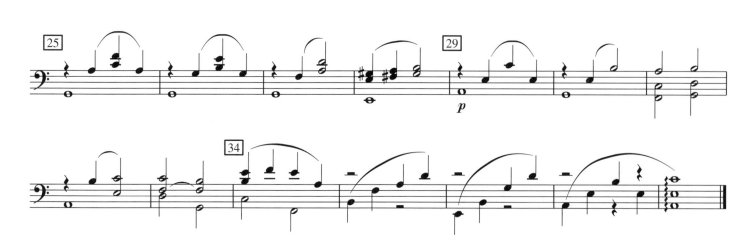

Monster March

By Jennifer Linn

Play both hands one octave lower.

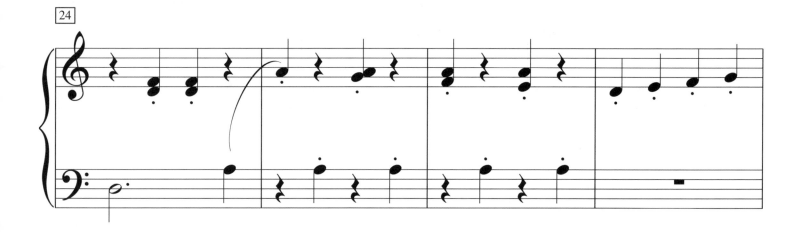

Play both hands two octaves lower to the end.

Party Cat Parade

Words and Music by
Jennifer Linn

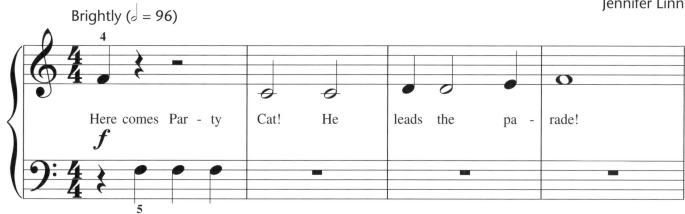

Brightly (♩ = 96)

Here comes Par - ty Cat! He leads the pa - rade!

Spike's at home, he's got a bone,'cause this pa - rade is just for kit - ties!

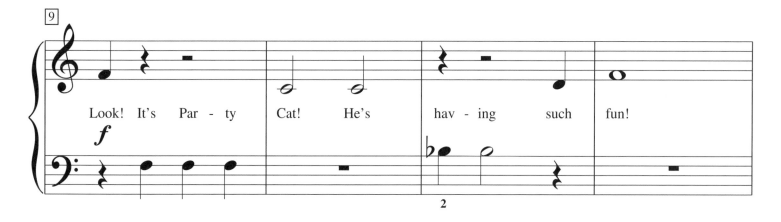

Look! It's Par - ty Cat! He's hav - ing such fun!

Accompaniment (Student plays one octave higher than written.)

Brightly (♩ = 96)

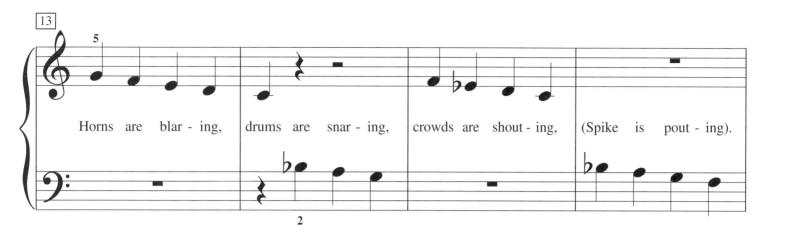

Horns are blar - ing, drums are snar - ing, crowds are shout - ing, (Spike is pout - ing).

Make way for Par - ty Cat's Pa - rade!

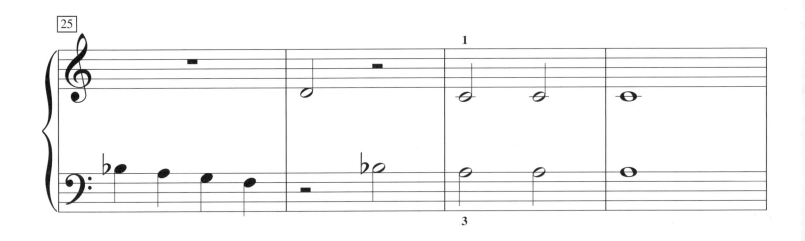

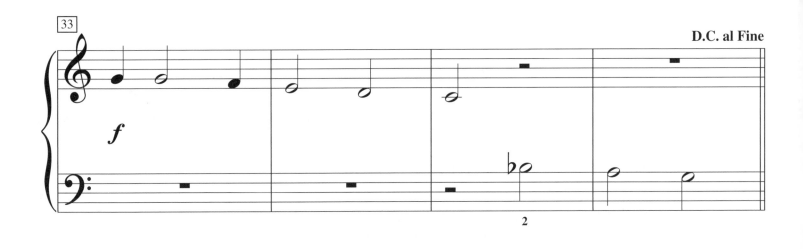

Rainy Day Play

Words and Music by
Carol Klose

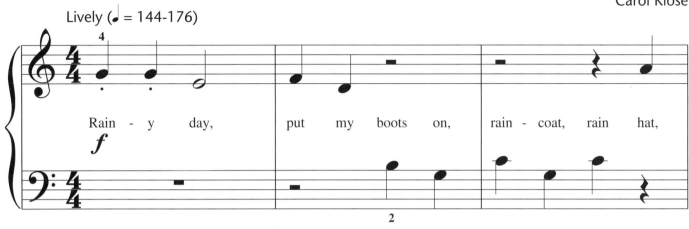

Rain - y day, put my boots on, rain - coat, rain hat,

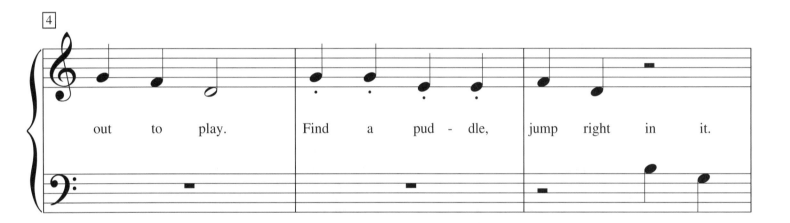

out to play. Find a pud - dle, jump right in it.

Accompaniment (Student plays one octave higher than written.)

Lively (♩ = 144-176)

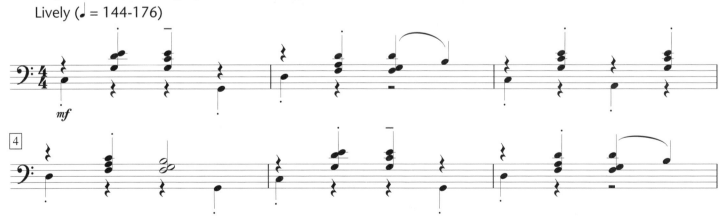

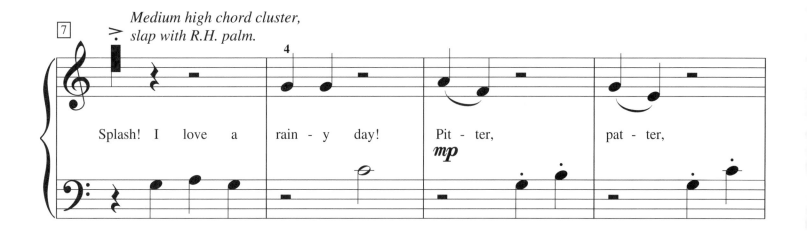

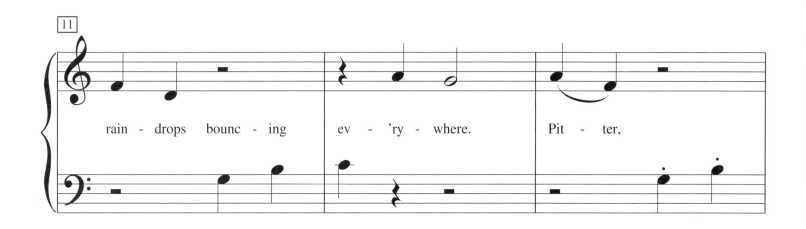

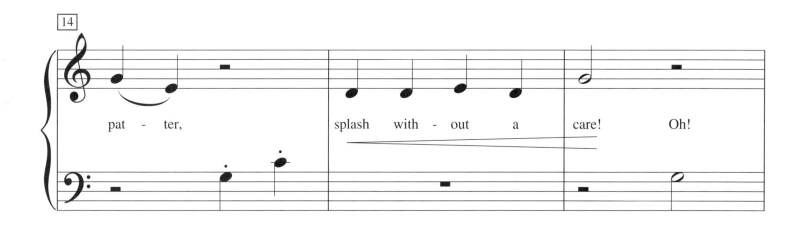

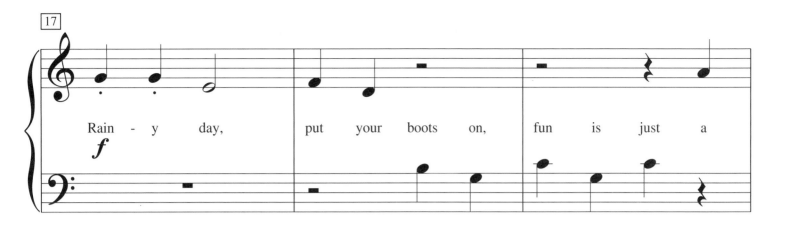

Rain - y day, put your boots on, fun is just a

splash a - way. Come with me and find a pud - dle.

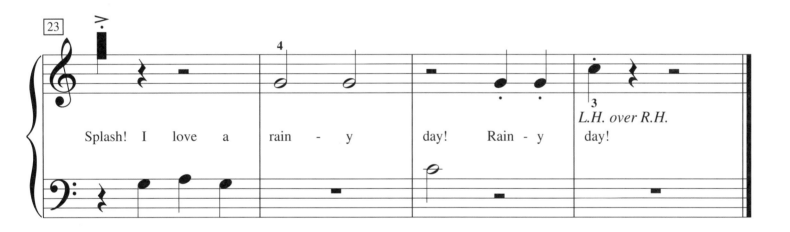

Splash! I love a rain - y day! Rain - y day!

L.H. over R.H.

Veggie Song

By Jennifer Linn

Moderately stubborn ($\quarternote$ = 184)

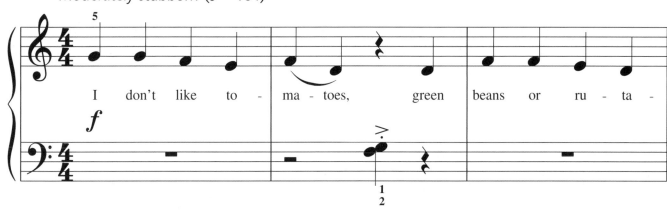

I don't like to - ma - toes, green beans or ru - ta -

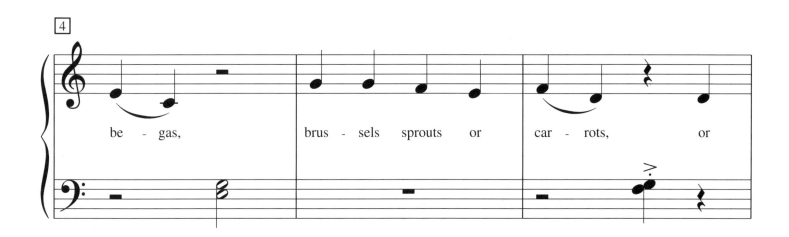

be - gas, brus - sels sprouts or car - rots, or

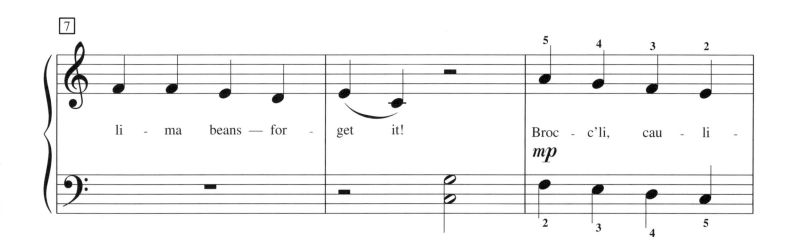

li - ma beans — for - get it! Broc - c'li, cau - li -

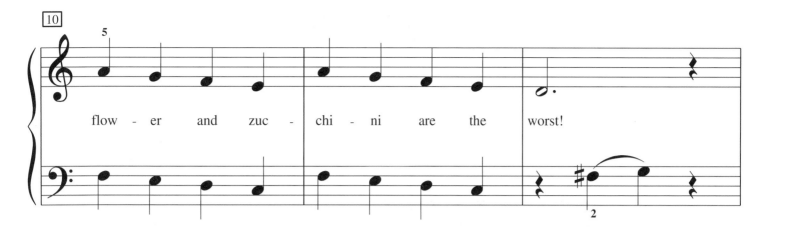

flow - er and zuc - chi - ni are the worst!

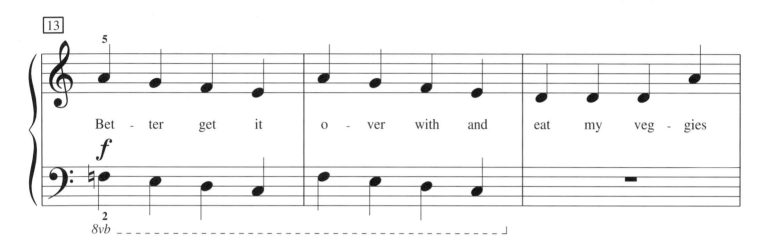

Bet - ter get it o - ver with and eat my veg - gies

first. I don't like to - ma - toes, green

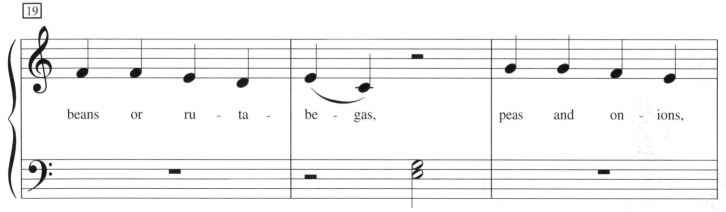

beans or ru - ta - be - gas, peas and on - ions,

spin - ach, too, re - mem - ber all these tastes are new!
rit.

Faster

If I have to try it, don't think that I will
a tempo

like it! Please make my serv - ing light and then I

f

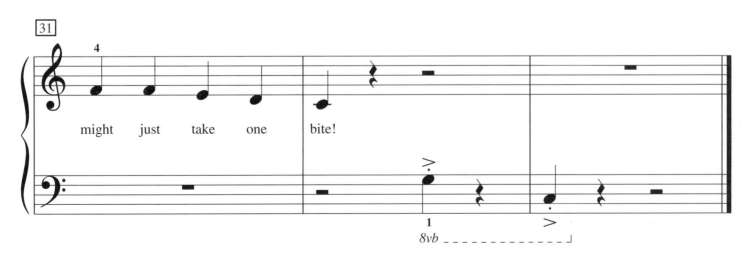

might just take one bite!

8vb